PIGS

FARM ANIMAL DISCOVERY LIBRARY

Lynn M. Stone

Rourke Corporation, Inc.
Vero Beach, Florida 32964

PHOTO CREDITS

All photos by the author

ACKNOWLEDGEMENTS

The author thanks the following for assistance in the
preparation of photos for this book: Howard, Becky, and
Laura Rosenwinkle, Big Rock, Ill.

LIBRARY OF CONGRESS
Library of Congress Cataloging-in-Publication Data
Stone, Lynn M.
   Pigs / by Lynn M. Stone.

   p. cm. — (Farm animal discovery library)
   Summary: An introduction to the physical characteristics,
habits, natural environment of pigs and their relationship
to humans.
   ISBN 0-86593-037-6
   1. Swine—Juvenile literature. [1. Pigs.] I. Title.
II. Series: Stone, Lynn M. Farm animal discovery library.
SF395.5.S76   1990
636.4—dc20   89-29873
                                   CIP
Printed in the USA   AC

A Piglet

TABLE OF CONTENTS

PIGS

The only part of a pig not used is its "oink." When a pig goes to market, every part of it is used. Pigs *(Sus scrofa)* are one of our most important animals.

Some of the first tame pigs were raised about 7,000 years ago in China. North America's first tame, or **domestic,** pigs were brought by Spanish explorers in the 1500's.

Pigs, also known as swine or hogs, have large **litters,** or groups of babies. They grow faster than other farm animals. And they eat almost anything.

Sow in mud

HOW PIGS LOOK

A pig is shaped like a barrel. It is covered with long, stiff hairs. A pig has short legs with sharp toes called hooves.

Its **snout** or nose is strong and flexible. The pig pokes its snout into the ground and **roots** for food.

Domestic pigs can be black, white, brown, reddish, or a mix of colors. Males may be four feet tall, six feet long, and weigh 800 pounds.

Boar drinking

WHERE PIGS LIVE

Pigs are raised in almost every country. The world has nearly 800 million pigs. China has the greatest number. For every five pigs in the world, China has two.

Russia is the world's second largest pig-producing country. The United States ranks third. Most pigs in North America are raised in the Midwest. There they are close to the corn that makes up most of their food.

Iowa raises more pigs than any other state, nearly 15 million.

Pigs love to soak

BREEDS OF PIGS

Almost all domestic pigs have the same family tree. They all began with the wild **boar.** Wild boars once lived on parts of three continents—Europe, Asia, and Africa.

Today there are many types, or **breeds,** of pigs. All breeds are the same basic animal. The differences show up on the animal's color and size and the amount of fat in the meat.

Eight breeds are commonly raised in the United States.

Hempshire boar

Piglets in a basket

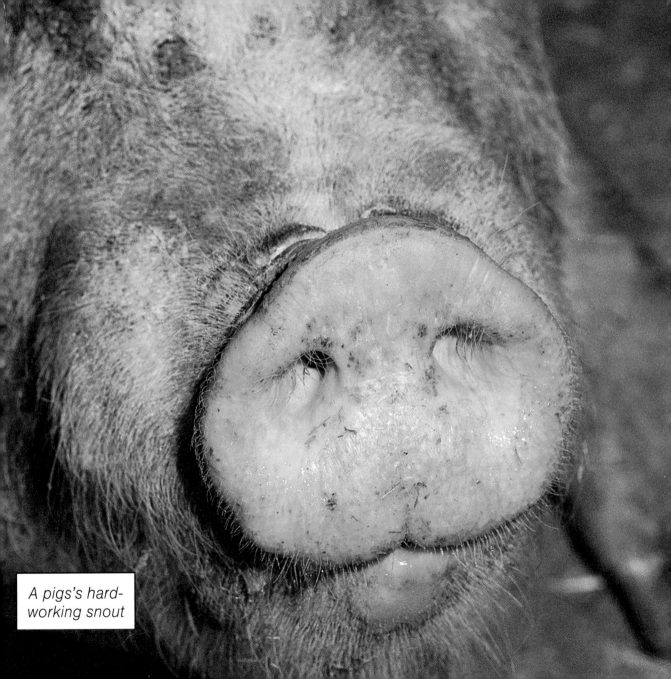

A pigs's hard-working snout

WILD PIGS

Stories describe pigs as fat and helpless. The eight kinds of wild pigs in the world are strong, quick, and often fierce.

The wild Javan pig, pygmy hog, bearded pig, and babirusa live in Asia. The bush pig, wart hog, and giant forest hog live in Africa.

The wild boar survives in bits of Europe and Asia.

Thousands of "wild pigs" live in California and the southeastern states. They are really domestic pigs whose ancestors escaped from farms.

Wild warthog in Africa

BABY PIGS

Pigs on modern American farms are born in pens with a heated sleeping area.

A mother pig, or **sow,** has a litter of six to twelve piglets. Each weighs about three pounds.

A pig can live to be nine or ten years old, but very few do. Most are taken to market at the age of six months. By then a pig weighs about 250 pounds.

Piglets nursing

HOW PIGS ARE RAISED

Farmers want pigs to grow quickly. They also want their pigs to have plenty of **lean** meat, which is meat with very little fat.

Most farmers limit the amount they feed pigs. Otherwise the pigs would eat too much and become fat.

Some pigs are kept indoors for their entire lives. Most, however, spend some time in outdoor pens or pastures. Pigs kept outdoors have shelters from the weather. White pigs can be sunburned.

A Midwest pig farm

HOW PIGS ACT

A person who eats too much has "pigged out." An idle person is "lazy as a pig." It is true that pigs are hearty eaters, and they often rest.

Pigs love to eat. They grunt and squeal as they gobble their feed.

A pig likes to nearly bury itself in mud or water. Mud is refreshing. Pigs also like to root in mud and scratch themselves on fence posts.

Pigs are one of the most intelligent domestic animals. They learn routines quickly and have good memories.

A pig rooting in mud

HOW PIGS ARE USED

The best-known use of hogs is for their meat, called **pork.** Some people eat fried hog intestines, or chitterlings. Hog kidneys, livers, ears, brains, and tongues are also eaten.

Hog skin is used for belts, gloves, wallets, and jackets. The hair is used for brushes and stuffing in baseball gloves and mattresses.

Pig blood and bones are used in animal feeds and fertilizers. Pig fat is used in soap, candles, oils, and shaving cream. The pig's "oink"? No one seems to know how to use that!

Glossary

boar (BORE)—a male pig; sometimes a wild pig native to Europe (wild boar, *Sus scrofa)*

breed (BREED)—closely related group of animals that came about through man's help; a type of domestic pig

domestic (dum ES tik)—tamed and raised by man

lean (LEEN)—mostly fat-free

litter (LITTER)—the group of babies born at the same time to a mother animal

pork (PORK)—the meat of pigs

root (ROOT)—to dig in and turn up the ground by using the nose or snout

snout (SNOUT)—the nose, especially of a pig

sow (SOW)—female pig

INDEX